Join in:

Breaking Tradition, Embracing Culture, Styles of Multicultural Worship

John Danso
Foreword by Francis Ackroyd

Published by

**MELROSE
BOOKS**

An Imprint of Melrose Press Limited
St Thomas Place, Ely
Cambridgeshire
CB7 4GG, UK
www.melrosebooks.com

FIRST EDITION

Copyright © John Danso 2009

The Author asserts his moral right to
be identified as the author of this work

Cover designed by Jeremy Kay

ISBN 978-1-906561-33-8

Printed and bound in Great Britain by:
the MPG Books Group

CONTENTS

Dedicated to a precious lifelong lover, comrade,
critic and wife, Mercy:
The constant, caring and enduring companion,
and spirited giver of steadfast love.

AND

My four angelic daughters, Evelyn, Cynthia, Ivy and
Stephanie, whom I love beyond measure and who remind
me daily, especially Stephanie, of the enduring beauty,
bounty and wonders of life on this earth.

ACKNOWLEDGEMENTS

Frustration, anxiety and concern were the motives that drove me in search of meaningful multicultural worship in British traditional churches. When I saw most of the ethnic minority people who worshipped as Presbyterians, Methodists, Catholics and Anglicans leave their churches to join self-styled Pentecostal churches, I thought, 'I have to do something about it'.

I therefore thank God for all the mercies shown to me in my search and the empowerment to finish this work.

I am most grateful to the Reverend Francis Ackroyd, whose guidance and direction helped to produce this book and the DVD. Reverend Dr Michael Jagessar was my supervisor who became a tower of strength for guiding me through from the beginning of this project to the end. Also Reverend Colin A. Smith, Superintendent of Barnet and Queensbury Circuit, and Reverend Dr Jeri-Jehu-Appiah who first read through the script for correction and advice. I thank my congregation at Trinity (Methodist/United Reformed Church) Golders Green for their support and prayers when I decided to work on the project. My thanks also go to the Reverend Fiona Thomas, Thames North Synod Training Officer, whose wisdom and direction helped me to focus on the project and to arrive at a final conclusion. My gratitude also goes to Katalina Tahaafe-Williams, United Reformed Church Secretary for Racial Justice and Multicultural Ministry, for taking time to look at the material and for her helpful suggestions.

I thank all the ministers, professors and principals of the-ological colleges in Bangalore in South India and South Africa whom I interviewed, and who are featured in the DVD. Thank you also to the Bishop of Kamataka Central Diocese of Churches of South India, and especially Mrs Patricia Job at the head office, who arranged and organised my activities while I was in Bangalore.

I am indebted to all the churches that helped me to conduct my search for multicultural worship and allowed me to film them. To all my friends and relatives who have contributed in many tangible ways, I convey my deepest gratitude.

Many, many thanks go to the Iona Community and Council for World Mission for the use of some of the choruses from their publication in this book. All rights are reserved.

"And we know that all things work together for good to those who love God, to those who are called according to His purpose."
(Romans 8:28)

FOREWORD

I have heard people in our churches say, 'What's the point of having disabled facilities when no disabled people ever come?' I wonder why? I have also heard people say, 'We don't know any young people so why can't we stay as we are and sing the hymns we like?' OK, so if we are a monocultural church, what's the point of multicultural worship?

As a minister who has served for nearly 40 years in the London area, first at Heaton Way on the Harold Hill housing estate in Romford, and then in Tottenham, I have seen communities change beyond recognition. Not only are most of our inner-city churches in multicultural communities, but also many churches, a considerable way out of London, are serving changing communities. The sad fact is, of course, that not all churches change with their communities. Some, however, do change and are enriched by the participation, gifts and talents of Caribbean and African roots, along with many other cultures. So let's not use the argument I began with, but be ready for change and new possibilities.

Secondly, we all belong to a global church, and many of us are involved for Life programmes and Fair Trade issues. We all belong to the Council for World Mission and benefit from this global family. Many of our churches are loyal participants in the Women's World Day of Prayer. So is it not natural and important to regularly use hymns and litanies from around the world, whatever the complexion of our congregation, to show we are serious about belonging to our global family?

Developing our worship in a multicultural way does not mean discarding everything we have used for a long time. It means helping everyone feel welcome and accepted as they are, and benefiting from the rich heritage and joy that other cultures bring. It also enables people from different cultural backgrounds to celebrate their spirituality within worship. With participation and respect we shall all grow in our worship of God.

The URC has declared itself a multicultural church and I commend John Danso's book and the DVD as a useful aid to all our churches who are willing to accept the present, and are open to God's challenge for the future.

Thank God for your inspiration and hard work.

Francis Ackroyd
Minister of High Cross URC, Tottenham

INTRODUCTION

This book is the result of my own experiences since I joined, and became a minister of, the United Reformed Church some years ago. The search for meaningful worship was a burden God laid on my heart. It has compelled me to search for ways of worship in multicultural communities that recognise and affirm their uniqueness and yet interconnectedness to other worshippers. In this way it liberates the minds of worshippers, which allows individuals the freedom to encounter God, and to freely express themselves before God.

My name is John Danso. I am Ghanaian-British (Black), a Liberal Theologian Minister of the United Reformed Church. At the time of writing, I was serving in the Methodist/United Reformed Church Golders Green

Pastorate. I combine both western and African theology to create what I call a multicultural theology. This is a new theological concept that is emerging to reflect the multicultural society in the twenty-first century in the western world. I joined the United Reformed Church many years ago. This was because the church I joined had about ten different nationalities and different cultures. I had the notion from the outset that the URC was a multicultural church. As I was soon to realise, however, the diversity of cultures was only incidental. In reality it did not matter or show in the way the particular congregation and its worship were styled. On the wider front, the URC hierarchy did not reflect the diversities in the Church, from the District Councils to the National Assembly.

I was very actively involved in the local church and district activities and events, so very quickly I was appointed as an elder of my local church. My active involvement in the United Reformed Church began one evening when the District Council was due to have one of its regular meetings in my local church. I volunteered to be on duty. This involved welcoming delegates, offering hospitality in the form of tea and coffee, and then later joining the meeting as an observer. I was very shocked to see that there was not a single ethnic minority person at the meeting. My shock was magnified by the knowledge that this is a district full of ethnic minority people in churches led by white ministers. I became aware that there were more ethnic minority elders in this particular district than in any other district in that synod. It became clear to me that their ministry did not go beyond the local church. I did research which led me to question many issues in the United Reformed Church in relation to ethnic minority members. This I recorded in my first book, *Ministry of Pastoral Care in Multicultural Churches* (available from the URC bookshop). I arranged to meet the then Moderator and confronted him with very challenging questions.

In addition to issues of ethnic minority representation at District Council and other councils of the United Reformed Church, there were also issues about worship styles in churches that appeared to be multicultural. I also struggled with the style of worship in most of the multicultural churches I have attended. Constantly I brought ideas for improving things. I knew what things I wanted to change, and why I wanted to change them. However, it was not as easy to determine what I should replace them with, or how to do it. I remained determined, however, to explore the field more rigorously, trusting the Holy Spirit to guide and inspire me. I needed to be grounded in my observations, fair in my criticisms, spiritual in my reading of events, and practical in my ideas. For me the over-riding objective was how to make church worship and church life generally a meaningful encounter with God for everybody. How to put my ideas across became a steep mountain to climb.

When I had the call to the Ministry, I was interviewed by fifteen White people who formed the District Pastoral Committee. As the years went by, and as one of the first African-British trained and ordained ministers in the United Reformed Church, my mind and my knowledge expanded in many different ways. I not only grew in my understanding of mission and theology, but I learnt and was exposed to ideas and to the discourse on notions of freedom, justice, democracy, human rights, equality and inclusiveness. I was caught up in a lasting and permanent search for universal truths, but was often in a fragile position, open to question and opposition because of the kind of person I am and/or what people perceived me to be.

Nonetheless, I held on to my ideas and one day I attended Cause for Celebration, which is an annual event organised by the Urban Churches Support Group to bring together people from different backgrounds. Representatives of all Churches in London, from Thames North and Southern Synods, attend this event. Sadly, those who attend are mostly black and ethnic minority members of the United Reformed Church. It does not appeal to the white members of the church. The celebration provides oppor-

4

tunities for people to share ideas and give support and encouragement to each other. A lasting and very positive outcome of this particular event was that it led to the General Assembly endorsing the move to publicly condemn racism and welcome diversity. The church agreed and adopted statements to challenge racism and to welcome diversity in the United Reformed Church. This later yielded a positive result when Marjorie Lewis-Cooper was appointed as the multiracial/multicultural field worker.

THE BOOK/DVD

I decided to use my sabbatical to explore how our churches, which are full of people from many different nationalities and cultures, reflect our multicultural and diverse world and society through worship. I embarked on a project to explore multiculturalism and diversity in the life and worship of the United Reformed Church. It was not my intention to produce a publication after I had taken up this project. However, as I got deeper into my research both here and abroad it became very clear to me that the styles of worship in our United Reformed Churches are not as accommodating of the spiritual needs of ethnic minority members as they could be. I was convinced that this is one key reason why many leave traditional and historic churches. This book and its accompanying DVD are aimed at promoting multicultural worship and encouraging ethnic minority groups in our churches. This resource is meant only as a guide to ministers and worship leaders for developing and enabling multicultural worship. It is not a prescriptive medicine, nor does it pretend to offer all answers to how multicultural worship can be done. The DVD is not a guide to what multicultural worship is; rather it gives you some examples of styles of multicultural worship.

WORSHIP

What is worship? Many writers, theologians and liturgists have written about it and offered various definitions. Many write from their specific religious perspectives, and there are a few very general ones. Churches have their own approved liturgies for worship and have offered what they understand and require of their congregations to practise as worship.

A useful starting point is to examine and compare what the churches have described as worship in their various worship books. I will start with my own denomination.

In the United Reformed Church worship book, a short preface written by John Huxtable[1] states that though the book is not prescriptive, yet they (the committee) believed most of these services reflect the ethos of our Church

---

1   *Worship from the United Reformed Church*, 2003

and of its traditions. In the same way the Methodists in their worship book[2] affirm that "Worship is a gracious encounter between God and the Church", the Anglicans[3] see their new and old books of worship as a liturgy which "belongs to a particular period and culture". All of them therefore see worship as an engagement of human beings with God. A question that arises is who are the people these worship books were designed for?

Join In not only explores different styles of worship but also tries to identify groups of people who seek through worship to encounter God. The act of worship in this sense is a collective enterprise, so that people are not only seeking an encounter with God, but are also encountering each other in various western traditions. In other words it is about multicultural worship.

WHAT IS MULTICULTURAL WORSHIP?

Try first to answer the following questions, then record your answers before you read on.

(a) Does your worship reflect the languages and cultures of your congregation and the surrounding community?

---

2 *The Methodist Worship Book*, 1999, p. vii
3 *The Alternative Service Book*, 1980, p. 9. Superseded by *Common Worship*, 2000

(b) Do you use more than one language during your worship?

(c) Do your Ministers/Worship Leaders have access to and use of multicultural resources?

(d) Do you welcome a variety of worship styles that draw on the experiences and practices of different ethnic groups whether or not your actual membership includes ethnic minority people?

(e) Do you provide your young people with opportunities to participate in, create and experience different worship styles?

(*Questions from a checklist: Urban Churches Support Group*)

Multicultural worship is worship by many different people, from different nationalities and cultures. They have come together as a congregation to worship, and to have an individual encounter with God. This experience is realised by their spiritual engagement, not only with God but by association with their fellow believers in the congregation through worshipful thoughts, words, choruses, hymns and silence.

This kind of worship which is planned for the congregation is experienced by individuals in their search for their spirituality. This, when repeated regularly throughout the year, offers them the hope of assurance and belonging. Multicultural worship offers individuals certain features, the deepest values of their spirituality, which link with their whole being and their sense of belonging. Multicultural worship is not the repetition of hasty, routine petitions or listening to mood-inducing music. It is the experience of being, where the worshipper is "lost in wonder, love, and praise", as expressed by Charles Wesley.

The Psalmist wrote, "I will praise You, O Lord, with my whole heart; I will tell of all your marvellous works" (*Psalms* 9:1). It is the awe of the individual that inspires adoration in their own mode. A multicultural congregation represents true disciples who have left all to join with other Christians, who feel they must obey the Lord's command of unbroken succession of discipleship. This obedience in the minds of individuals becomes the foundation stone upon which the structure of multicultural worship is built. They come together to join in to glorify Christ's love, grace and mercy. Thus, the great command: "Go therefore and make disciples of all nations …" (*Matthew* 28:19*ff*). This reminds individual Christians, wherever they have come from, to recognise where others have come from, being drawn together by that same saving message of our Lord Jesus Christ. That is to assemble and to offer meaningful worship to God. Multicultural worship therefore springs from the great command.

The liturgy and all that is involved in multicultural worship – music, choruses, hymns, prayers, preaching the word of God etc. – are expressions of the presence of the Holy Spirit. The liturgy is an expression of faith and fellowship among different people from different cultural backgrounds proclaiming the divine means of Grace that is showered upon them. This expression in multicultural worship shows the obedience of individual Christians to the way of life of true disciples.

When individuals who are already committed disciples travel away from their original place of birth, as refugees, asylum seekers or economic migrants, the first thing on their minds is a place where they would be welcome to join in to worship God. Multicultural worship is thus not only a celebration by worshippers of God's abundance and grace, and an act of communion with Him, but is also a commitment to the communion with fellow believers. In their communion together, sincere thoughts of God and the presence of the Holy Spirit bind them to one another as brothers and sisters in Christ.

David Peel, in his book *Encountering Church*, reminds us that the Jerusalem church remained Jewish, but they added the rather distinctive practice of what is called "breaking bread" to their worship. The breaking of bread represented the sharing of commonality as souls seeking redemption and expressing a faith in the risen Lord, be they Jewish or Gentile, slave or free. Multicultural worship brings us together to share fellowship in a meaningful way to fulfil the command of Jesus, that all may be one. As humans we are defined by many realities, including our cultures. The Holy Spirit, the presence of God, subsumes all the different identities, but does not dissolve them. As observed by David Peel, therefore, we need "to create patterns of worship which meet the needs of different ages, temperaments and tastes".[4] Multicultural worship is a collection of individual people from different cultural backgrounds, sharing with others in a worship that is meaningful to them, giving those individuals their inspiration through being fully incorporated in the worship.

MEANINGFUL WORSHIP

Multicultural worship is to do with breaking tradition and embracing culture into the liturgy of worship. It is a way of worship that is meaningful to the individual in particular and the whole congregation in general. It is the way the

---

4   David Peel, *Encountering Church*, 2006, p. 51

whole congregation becomes *enculturated*. Enculturation is a word I came across in India during my sabbatical. It is used by the National Biblical Catechetical and Liturgical Centre which belongs to the Catholic Church. The centre has embraced the Indian culture in everything they do during worship time. The word therefore means bringing together different aspects of their cultures into their worship.

This kind of worship has three dimensions: the past, the present and the future. Britain is rapidly becoming a multicultural country, but London is already a multicultural city. It has become and will remain like that till the end of time. London therefore needs a new theology of worship. As the churches aspire to be multicultural, the real challenge it presents is the breaking of the present day Eurocentric style of worship, and the incorporation of many cultural styles into the worship, maintaining, nevertheless, the church's solid foundation and traditions.

ETHNIC

The word "ethnic" comes from the Greek word *ethnikos* and refers to a people or a nation. The *Concise Oxford Dictionary* states that an ethnic group is a social group of people who have a common national or cultural tradition, denoting origin by birth or descent rather than nationality, which is related to race or culture.

The term "ethnic minority" is usually used to refer to an identifiable group of people differentiated from the main population of a community by racial origin or cultural background.

CULTURE

A dictionary meaning is "the customs, civilization and achievement of a particular people". The word is used to describe the attitudes, values and ways of life of a particular group of people who share common goals. People who migrate to other countries go with their culture. Where there are more people from the same area they join together to practise their culture in their daily lives. The members of the group do things together to create their identity. In a community there may be different groups of people with different cultures.

The word **MULTICULTURAL**, therefore, means many or several cultures or ethnic groups living within a society.

DIFFERENT ORDERS

In multicultural worship any liturgy used must allow each individual the freedom to worship God and not be restricted. Different orders of service will not prevent any individual during the process of worship from engaging with God.

My sabbatical took me to Churches in South India, the Karnataka Diocese and to the Uniting Presbyterian Church in Southern Africa. I was amazed but at the same time shocked in many ways. There are many churches which are expressing their cultures in their worship. They offer individuals the opportunity to engage freely and personally with their God. They are maintaining the past tradition, but at the same time using their drums and their lyrics to grace the worship. My experiences in such churches is that they feel comfortable as they sit on the mats on the floor and sing their own lyrics. One could observe that they are indeed being connected spiritually with their God. However, there are few who continue to worship in what was described by the clerk of the Uniting Presbyterian Churches of South Africa as "the hymn sandwich service". In such services, they have restricted orders of service which, from my observation, restrict most individuals from having meaningful worship.

In some of the Uniting Presbyterian Churches of South Africa where there are mixed multi-ethnic congregations, there are three different kinds of hymn books. The hymns are written in their local languages: Zulu, Xhosa and Sotho. The minister-in-charge informed me that every week they sing from all the hymn books. This allows individual tribal groups to belong to and be part of the worship, because they are able to use their own language to sing and to praise God during worship. The minister does not preach in one language each week. He tries to preach in alternate languages each week, to be translated. This and my other experiences of worship have inspired me to produce four models of worship under various headings.

ORDER OF SERVICE

WELCOME

In multicultural worship it is very important to extend a personal welcome to all those who are present if possible. Let people be aware that their presence is known and they are warmly welcome to worship with others.

HYMNS OR CHORUSES

Hymns or choruses play an important part in multicultural worship. They are used to praise God and to draw individuals, through their singing, closer to God. If there are choruses, more than one may be sung to allow people time to prepare or warm up to engage with God. One must feel free to use old ones and learn new ones every time.

METHODS OF PRAYER

(*All prayers in the DIFFERENT ORDER models are simple words used by individuals when they are asked to pray during worship.*)

For most, if not all, who come to church, their main purpose is to come and pray to God personally. All prayers need to be personal. The individual has come to ask personal forgiveness from God. They have come to talk to God personally. Therefore in multicultural worship prayers need to address individual needs.

Among the gathering there may be asylum seekers who have been tortured and are fleeing from persecution, people who have been raped and need some reassurance, refugees who are struggling to survive, divorced men and women, families who are facing all sorts of problems. All these people are there to ask God to help them to come to terms with their various situations.

When the time comes to pray in multicultural worship, there should sometimes be an opportunity for individuals to spontaneously pray aloud in their own languages. This kind of prayer is led by the minister or worship leader, who announces selected topics upon which the individuals pray. This will allow individuals to attempt to talk to their God personally in any language they choose. This could be during confession of sins or intercessory prayers. Like children, many worshippers in a multicultural service may prefer to talk to God as they talk to their parents at home. People need to have the real opportunity and the heart to go to God to pray in their own words. Often people pray to God by using simple words to address their needs.

There should also sometimes be time for silent prayers. This is very important to some people who will fail to achieve anything or address their fullest spiritual needs without it. The use of silent prayer will help them keep before their minds the true nature of the Christian ideal of conduct as revealed by our Lord Jesus who on many occasions retreated to be silent. Silent prayer reveals to us the ever-increasing extent of our sins and failures, and how we could overcome them. It also adds fresh meaning and life to our vocal mass prayers and our attendance at worship. This kind of prayer helps us to abstain from formal and lifeless repetitions of words which have no spiritual meaning.

TESTIMONY

In multicultural worship there should also sometimes be time for individuals to offer their own testimonies. There is a desire in many people to be given the opportunity to thank God for what He has done for them. This could be a miraculous saving or deliverance or an answered prayer. This kind of testimony encourages others and ministers to them in many ways. It should be encouraged as part of our mission work.

SERMONS

The first priority of most worshipers is to hear the word of God. This said, the manner of communicating the word of God should not be restricted to formal preaching all the time. There are other ways of expression that are equally effective, if not more so, in sharing the word of God in worship.

It is very important to vary the sermons occasionally to allow discussions, reflections and the gaining of bible knowledge. Multicultural worship is far more than a collective of personal interest in the abstract and the absolute. It rather gives a united testimony to the world and provides spiritual development for all those who have gathered. The word, in whichever form it comes, becomes the power of edification. Deliberation upon deliberation, teaching upon teaching, the word of God comes into the hearts and minds of many. This gives practical challenges for life and powerful motives for living. The way the word of God is presented during worship needs to relate to life (contextual). In the liturgy models you will realise different activities that can take place when the time comes for the proclamation of the word.

BIBLE READINGS

During multicultural worship the use of dramatised Bible readings is highly recommended. This encourages individual participation in the worship.

OFFERTORY

Passing collection bags around is the traditional way of giving in the church, which could be changed occasionally in multicultural worship. Members may be asked to bring their offerings forward to a bowl placed in front of the altar. Mark 12:41 clearly reminds us that offertories are brought forward to be put in a bowl, rather than being collected. During this time, lively music is played, or a song or a chorus is sung as members come to bring their offerings.

NOTICES

When the notice of the week is read, greetings must be extended to all people, but especially to those who are attending for the first time. They may be requested to stand up and introduce themselves, and offered a formal welcome. They may be asked if they are visitors or have just moved to the area. If there is time they may be invited forward and the minister may shake hands with them. They may be offered the opportunity after the service to meet an elder or a pastoral leader, who may take their details for follow-up contacts. The congregation should be asked if it is someone's birthday, and let the whole congregation join together to sing a happy birthday song for them. It will also be appreciated if cards are presented to them, especially the children and youths.

SO WHAT IS *JOIN IN*?

The models of multicultural worship presented in this book are nothing more than an enrichment of the Western style of worship. They are intended to help accommodate the influx of immigrants who join congregations to worship with them. By using them, we create an atmosphere that enables people to feel that they are really part of the church and its worship rather than just guests.

Join In describes different models of service that include the participation of individuals and people from ethnic minority groups in worship. This incorporates their songs, music and other meaningful expressions, so as to offer them a form of worship that will make them really encounter God. This kind of worship then becomes, as Pete Ward describes, a solid church.[5] It should not be a church where those in charge think one size fits all. It should not be one where on each Sunday, worship is designed to make everyone think and feel that, even if they do not like everything, they should be glad that others can fully participate.

Join In is not only a book but comes with a DVD. The book may be meaningless to you unless you first watch the DVD, which gives you a taste of what multicultural

---

5   Pete Ward, *Liquid Church*, Hendrickson Publishers, USA, 2002, p. 19

worship looks like. It also informs you, through various interviews, of the importance and the need for multicultural churches to develop a new style of worship in our twenty-first century. The models are not prescriptive. One can choose and mix from any of the models to suit the needs of any congregation.

My prayer is that this book and DVD may be of value to all ministers, worship leaders and all local churches in helping their multicultural congregations have meaningful worship. It is my genuine desire that all multicultural congregations, as well as monocultural congregations, who meet to confess and proclaim the Lord Jesus Christ, can foster an atmosphere of freedom in which they can worship freely and still maintain their membership in the local churches.

At the end of the book are thirty choruses chosen from other parts of the world to help promote the styles of multicultural worship.

LITURGY MODEL ONE

INTRODUCTION

Some of the elements of this model may seem familiar to you. The additions to it are intended to enrich the service, and to create an atmosphere conducive to multicultural worship. This model may be used in a congregation where there are one or two ethnic minority groups. The service may start with praises, singing choruses to prepare the congregation for the main service. A member who knows the choruses may be asked to lead the singing, even teach them to the rest of the congregation where necessary. Ethnic minority individuals could sing a solo in their own language.

All the models offer different ways in which our Sunday offerings are given. Instead of waiting for someone to come round to collect, members dance to music and bring their offerings forward to place them in a bowl at the front of the Church (see *Mark* 12: 41-42).

The models offer the ethnic minority people in the congregation the opportunity to participate in the worship. The prayers of intercession are personal. When praying for the heads of states, ethnic minority member countries' heads of states' names should be mentioned in the prayers. This makes all members of the congregation feel that they also belong.

The structure of the following liturgy models may seem too traditional to some, and contrary to what multicultural worship should be. My focus has been more on content than structure. My aim is to give worship leaders enough content to help in the actual act of worship so as to enable multicultural expression and participation. I would encourage any group or church using these models to adapt them to suit their particular content.

LITURGY MODEL
(Before the worship begins)

INVOCATION
Let the congregation sing some choruses, offering God a time of praise and allowing individuals the opportunity to

glorify God before the worship starts. (There is a choice of choruses and hymns at the back of the liturgies.)

CALL TO WORSHIP
(Appropriate selected text of the day)

OR:

> *Come all you who have gathered here today,*
> *Come and let us worship the Lord our God.*
> *Come let us praise the Almighty and creator of*
> *the universe,*
> *Come let us glorify Jesus Christ, the source of*
> *abundant life.*
> *Come all of you; let us celebrate the presence of*
> *the Holy Spirit,*
> *The One who guides and directs a meaningful*
> *life.*

WELCOME

Greetings. May I take this opportunity to welcome you all to this place of worship. This is God's house, and if today is your first time here, feel at home, and if you have already made this place your home, then let us all join to worship God.

HYMN OR CHORUS

OPENING PRAYERS

ADORATION

Almighty Father, Mother, our creator, maker of Heaven
and Earth, our protector from all evil, our advocate,
counsellor, giver of hope and assurance, the one triune
God: we adore your name and your presence with us
here today. Join us in worship and enable us through the
Holy Spirit to feel your presence with us throughout the
service.

THANKSGIVING

The following thanksgiving may be spoken as "I" rather
than "we" if appropriate. The same applies to most of the
spoken pieces in these liturgy models.

Most gracious and loving God, we offer our sincere thanks to you as we have gathered to worship
you. We thank you for caring for us throughout
the deepest night and making us see yet another
day.

We thank you for your guidance and for bringing
us here today to worship you.

We thank you for the food, clothes, and the blessings you have showered upon us.

We thank you for our parents, guardians and for giving them the love to care for us.

We thank you for making it possible for us to come to your Church to worship you today. Come among us and continue to renew us minute by minute in your presence. We ask these through Jesus Christ your Son.

INVITATION TO CONFESSION OF SIN
Invite the congregation to remain silent for a moment to prepare their hearts to pray. Again, the following invitation may be spoken as "I" rather than "we" if appropriate.

Loving and caring God, we know you are present to hear us as we confess our sins to you in honesty. You know us more than we know ourselves. We have not loved the person sitting next to us as we ought to.

Lord, we ask you wholeheartedly to forgive us.

We have used words that hurt to describe others, to insult others, to belittle others.

Lord, forgive us.

We have made someone we know sad, we have failed to value those we know, and failed to value those we do not know, because of their colour and gender.

Lord, forgive us.

Help us to recognise genuinely all our faults and not to repeat them over again.

Help us to love all people whom we will meet today without discrimination or prejudice, but truly and earnestly, as we love you.

We thank you for touching us at this moment and for relieving us of all our wrongdoings.

Compassionate God; reconcile us anew, through our Lord Jesus Christ now and evermore. Amen.

We say the prayer our Lord taught us. Our father...

HYMN OR SONG

(Led by individuals, or choirs, or group of people)

BIBLE READING
(Dramatised Bible may be used)
At the end of the reading:
This is the word of God
Thanks be to God

HYMN OR CHORUS

TESTIMONY
If you wish to introduce testimony time, announce this a week before to prepare those who wish to share their faith with others.

Offer individuals the opportunity to participate by inviting those who want to thank God for what He has done for them to do so. This could be a miraculous saving or deliverance or an answered prayer. Testimonies should encourage others and build up the faith of the whole church. They should be short and to the point. This kind of testimony encourages others and ministers to them in many ways.

PRAYER OF INTERCESSION

The minister/leader invites the congregation to prayer with the following words:

> Let us come together with one heart and with one mind to pray together for others and for ourselves. Let us remain silent for a moment.

These Prayers should be personalised.

> Most gracious and loving God, you have always asked us to come to you with our concerns. Hear us as we bring before you our prayers.

> Let us all join together to pray for the Church we belong to and pray for all churches in our community and churches all over the world.

> Fill our church with the Holy Spirit to enable us to feel your presence each time we come here. Let your loving peace dwell upon us always.

> We pray that churches in our community may be one and that all churches around the world may continue to proclaim the good news with their lives to all people.

(Silence)

Almighty Father, with your presence around the world, we ask your everlasting wisdom upon those whom you have chosen to lead your Church and to care for those who worship in it.

Grant grace and wisdom to all ministers but especially our minister (name), our moderators and especially (name) of (name) Synod.

Shower your blessings upon all leaders of the church, elders, pastoral leaders, junior church leaders, leaders of all committees, that they may have joy and love to carry out their duties.

(Silence)

Creator of the universe, we ask you to grant wisdom to those who have been elected to bear authority all over the world: to cater for the affairs of human beings, especially (names of presidents, kings or queens, prime ministers of countries represented at the church), in addition to all those who serve with them; that they may govern with justice and honour.

(Silence)

Loving God, we now bring before you the concerns of your people whom you have called to serve you. Let us at this moment ask God to touch ...

People who have been tortured ...

(Silence)

People who have been raped ...

(Silence)

People who are fleeing from persecution and have left their loved ones behind ...

(Silence)

People who have experienced any form of abuse and are still carrying their pain and anger with them at this moment ...

(Silence)

Father, you who care for your children, help them

now, hug them, embrace them, and assure them that they are not alone.

(Silence)

Touch also those who are experiencing problems in their marriages, people who have experienced bitter divorce, to remind them that you are always present with them.

(Silence)

Most gracious and loving God, You said: "Let the little children come to me, and do not stop them; for it is to such as these that the kingdom of heaven belong" (Matthew 19:14).

We therefore bring to you the care of our children and youths. Touch them as they worship you. Help them to discern your ways and how to conduct their lives as they grow. Help individual children who have not been obedient to their parents or carers. Lord, touch them and give them a sense of belonging.

Help parents and carers to have patience and tolerance for the child that stands in front of them.

Let them offer this child a hand full of unconditional love, full of hope and assurance.

(Silence)

Help the young adults who are looking for wives and husbands, that they meet the right persons who will offer them love similar to that you give to your children. Always assure them of your presence when they call on you.

(Silence)

Heavenly Father, healer and sustainer of life, we offer to you at this moment the sick, the terminally ill, those in pain and those who are here among us ...

(Silence or names of individuals may be called)

Those who are not here with us but request your touch as they lie in their homes, hospital beds, those who are suffering with pain ...

(Silence)

Those who are depressed and feel life is not worth living …

(Silence)

Those who are poor and struggling to provide daily bread for their families, the homeless who seek a warm place to lay their head …

(Silence)

Those who are looking for work to be able to support their family …

(Silence)

Touch them and let them feel your presence with assurance that they are not alone.

(Silence)

Eternal Lord, you have assured us that in your Father's house there are many dwelling places (John 14:2), and so we are certain that our loved ones who have faithfully left us on this earth are comfortably with you. Help us to follow their good examples, until you call us to become members of your heavenly household.

Lord Almighty Father, thank you for sharing with us our concerns. Continue to unload our burdens as we always walk with you in our daily lives.

Amen.

During the prayer of intercession, a prayerful hymn or chorus may be played as background music, e.g. "I need thee every hour" or "Jesu tawapano" (from choruses at the end of the book).

HYMN OR CHORUS

BIBLE READING
This may be read as in the dramatised version of the Bible by different people.

(At the end of the Reading)
This is the word of God
Thanks be to God

SERMON
The sermon may take different forms. There are four different models:

1. Preaching the word of God.
2. Bible discussion in small groups. The groups

will depend on the size of the congregation. If you intend using this model, then you need to prepare in advance questions on the text and give them to group leaders to facilitate the discussion. There should be feedback from the groups. The minister/worship leader sums up to conclude this model.

Example 1:
Bible study at morning service instead of preaching
Occasion: Racial Justice Sunday
Text: Luke chapter 10:25-37
Theme: Who am I?

Guidance notes:
Try to encourage everyone in your group to say something. Let them bring out their views, and how they understand the passage.

Due to time limit, avoid one person dominating. Read the passage aloud.

You have twenty minutes (this could vary).

Record important points for feedback.

Use the following as a guide:

(a) What is/are the main point/s in the story? For example, identity – where do you come from, are you different from others? In what ways?

(b) What are PREJUDICE and RACISM?

(c) How can Christians avoid them?

(d) Are we different from refugees, settlers, asylum seekers?

(e) What commitment and action should we take to avoid Racism and Prejudice in our church?

Come back with your group for feedback. Write important points on a flip-chart. Summarise and continue with the service.

Example 2:
Bible study at morning service instead of preaching

Guidance notes:
Try to encourage everyone in your group to say something. Let them bring out their views, and how they understand the passage.

Due to time limit, avoid one person dominating. Read the passage aloud.

You have twenty minutes (this could vary).

Record important points for feedback.

Use the following as a guide:

Text: *Matthew* 13:1-9, 18-23

Theme: Where did I fall?

(a) Which part of the reading is most likely to speak to you directly?

(b) What do you think it would say to you?

(c) Are there any parts of this passage you would find difficult in any way?

(d) What do you think God might be saying to you through this passage?

(e) Imagine that this passage did speak to you profoundly. How might you act?

Come back with your group for feedback. Write important points on a flip-chart. Summarise and continue with the service.

3. Dramatised play by group of ethnic people or children etc.

4. Instead of a sermon, invite two or three people from the congregation to contribute short addresses attempting to say:

   i. How the Christian faith supports, guides, directs or challenges them in their lives, especially in their workplaces.

   ii. What Christian insights are helpful in their daily work; how they may see their Christian responsibilities as managers, cleaners, supervisors, teachers, receptionists, etc.

   iii. What are the most tempting and difficult areas in their workplaces? Where and when do they seek God's guidance?

(Those contributing must be informed beforehand; and if this method will be used, make an announcement the week before.)

NOTICES

Extend greetings to all people but especially those who are attending for the first time. Request them to stand up and let them introduce themselves. Are they visitors or have they just moved to the area? Offer them the opportunity after the service to meet an elder or a pastoral leader to take their details. Also, enquire from the congregation if it is someone's birthday. Join together to sing "Happy Birthday".

OFFERTORY

Members may be asked to bring their offerings forward into a bowl placed in front of the altar. Lively music is played, or a song or a chorus is sung, as members dance to bring their offerings.

OFFERTORY PRAYER

HYMN OR CHORUS

BENEDICTION

LITURGY MODEL TWO

INTRODUCTION

Model two offers the opportunity for ethnic minority people in the congregation to engage with their God in their own time during worship. It allows people to pray aloud in their own language; this, for most people, helps them to pour out their soul to God. It allows them to sing choruses in their own language, which prepares them to meet God. The model also tells others through their testimonies the wonders and miracles God has done through their belief. The model offers the minister and worship leaders different ways of understanding and presenting scriptures.

The model invites individuals who have something to contribute to make the worship meaningful to them and the whole congregation. It becomes a personal testimony to them. It also helps them to engage personally with God. The model helps those taking part to allow the Spirit to inspire them, and gives them the freedom to engage personally with God.

LITURGY MODEL

CALL TO WORSHIP

INTROIT
(A chorus by an individual or choir)

WELCOME

Today is a day of rest for Christians. You have made it a duty to come and worship your God. Let me take this opportunity to welcome you personally to God's house. I welcome both old members, who worship here each Sunday, and any new member who has joined us today. Once you are here, let me assure you that you are not a stranger but a member of God's kingdom. Therefore, feel free and at home and enjoy every bit of your presence here with God and fellow Christians.

HYMN OR CHORUS
There is a choice of choruses at end of book to choose from. Alternatively, a hymn can be sung.

OPENING PRAYER
(Invitation to pray)

> *Let us come to God with one mind and with one heart to pray to Him. Loving God, offer us serenity of the mind as we bring our thanks to you.*

THANKSGIVING/ADORATION

> *Most gracious and Loving God, we thank you for all the blessings you have showered upon us.*

> *We thank you for your great glory, Most Heavenly Father.*

> *We thank you for guiding us throughout this night, and for the opportunity to see another day.*

> *We thank you for our health and strength, for the food and clothes you have given us.*

> *We thank you for the air we breathe, for our families, our friends and neighbours, and for the community in which we belong.*

> *We thank you for all the little and great things that you have done for us throughout our lives.*

We thank you for all the good things that we have enjoyed.

We thank you also for all the disappointments in our lives, which have made us ungrateful to you. Continue, Almighty God, with your love and mercy to feed us with your abundant grace and joy. Let us always remember that you are there to give when we ask in your name.

CONFESSION OF SIN

Let us in genuineness come before you, most gracious God, to confess the sins that we have committed against you.

(Silence)

Most Holy God, here we are in front of you in humbleness, asking you to forgive us for a particular sin we have inflicted upon a neighbour, a friend, a member of the congregation, consciously or unconsciously. Help us not to repeat it again.

(Silence)

Almighty God, we have not loved you as we ought

to. We have not given you time as we give to other activities; we have in most cases failed to read your word and pray as we ought to. For all these years we have called upon your name, Christ, but have not departed from our dark path; instead we have taken you for granted and used your name, Christ, for our own gain. Please forgive us.

(Silence)

Bring our minds and thoughts together this moment as we worship you. Be present with us throughout the time we will spend here today. We ask these things through Jesus Christ our Lord and Saviour. Amen.

HYMN OR CHORUS

SONG/ANTHEM

This could be by an individual, a group of people or the choir.

BIBLE READING

The reading may be read by individuals or a group of adults or children (if children are present) in dramatised form.

(At the end of the reading)
This is the word of God
Thanks be to God

HYMN OR CHORUS

TESTIMONY

If you wish to introduce testimony time, announce this a week before to prepare those who wish to share their faith with others.

Invite individuals who want to thank God for what God has done for them. This could be a miraculous saving or deliverance or an answered prayer. Testimonies should encourage others and build up the faith of the whole church. They should be short and to the point. This kind of testimony encourages others, and ministers to them in many ways.

PRAYER OF INTERCESSION

The minister/worship leader prepares the congregation for an open vocal prayer.

Let us come together with one mind and one heart to pray for ourselves and others. You will be invited to pray aloud in any language during the prayers. Let's remain silent for a moment.

Silence is kept for a while.

The minister/worship leader reads out the topics to be prayed about. You may choose to put one or two together or one after the other.

(a) Invite someone to pray for churches all over the world, but especially our church here in (*name*) and all local churches.

(b) Invite another person to pray for all those who proclaim the word of God. Our minister (*name*) the moderator (*name*), the elders and leaders of all committees.

(c) Invite another person to pray for our Sunday school teachers, all the children who attend, and the Youth for God to give them love and understanding; for parents and carers, and families that are going through difficult times.

(d) Invite another person to pray for the sick, the suffering, the homeless, the hungry, the orphans, widows and widowers, refugees and asylum seekers; those who have been raped or tortured and those who are facing pain from divorce.

(e) Invite another person to pray for peace in the world, for an end to wars that displace innocent people. Pray for (*names of prime ministers or presidents of countries represented in the church if known*) and all people who are involved in bringing peace to the world.

(f) Invite another person to pray for their families, and especially the children who have been left behind.

(g) At this point invite individuals to bring their own personal requests before God. Bring before God in silence your own concerns. Pray to God in silence. Put before him your requests and He is willing to answer them for you.

The minister/worship leader concludes prayer with the following words:

Most gracious and loving God, we thank you for hearing our prayers. Continue to keep us under your umbrella and guard us through our lives. Amen.

This should be followed by the Lord's Prayer if not already said.

HYMN OR CHORUS

READING
(At the end of the reading)
This is the word of God
Thanks be to God

SERMON
Choose from the following options.

(a) Preaching the word of God.

(b) Bible study in small groups. If you choose to use this option then you need to choose the text and prepare questions (examples in Liturgy Model One) and choose group leaders to facilitate discussion. Round up the study with either feedback from the groups or a summary from the minister/worship leader.

(c) Instead of a sermon, invite two or three people from the congregation (they must be informed beforehand, perhaps by making an announcement a week before) to contribute short addresses attempting to say:

i. How the Christian faith supports, guides, directs or challenges them within the sphere of their lives; especially in their workplaces.

ii. What Christian insights are helpful in their daily work; how they may see their Christian responsibilities as managers, supervisors, teachers, receptionists, cleaners etc.

iii. What are the most tempting and difficult areas, as Christians, in their workplaces.

iv. Where and when they seek God's guidance.

PRAYER

This may be a silent prayer after the sermon or Bible study, or a vocal prayer by the minister/worship leader.

NOTICES

Extend greetings to all people but especially those who are attending for the first time. Request them to stand up and let them introduce themselves. Are they visitors or have they just moved to the area? Offer them the opportunity after the service to meet an elder or a pastoral leader to take their details. Also, enquire from the congregation if it is someone's birthday. Join in singing "Happy Birthday" for them.

OFFERTORY
Members may be asked to bring their offerings forward to a bowl placed in front of the altar. Lively music is played, or a song or a chorus is sung, as members dance to bring their offerings.

OFFERTORY PRAYER

HYMN OR CHORUS

BENEDICTION

LITURGY MODEL THREE

INTRODUCTION

This model offers three different activities to start the worship. The model is to offer ethnic minority people the opportunity to explore their own spirituality in depth. Here I mean to say that they are given the freedom to engage with the spirit of devotion and the desire for common communion with God.

The model offers opportunities in the worship for members to explore the Bible and also allows individuals to give testimonies to acknowledge God's activity in their lives, to provide a heightened awareness for each and all who have gathered to worship God.

During the worship, people are led to pray in their own time, to offer a real means of accessing the Grace of God. This helps those who are engaged in their own prayers to relate the worship to real life. Attention is given to singing and praising God in different languages, the challenges of their faith in their daily lives, and meaningful ceremonies that involve all people in the congregation. There is emphasis on teaching the essential truths of Christianity using different approaches, with the objective of leading both young and old, men and women, into the full appreciation of being a member of a multicultural church that has faith and is alive.

The model will offer meaningful worship only if people are fully involved in the worship.

LITURGY MODEL

BEFORE CALL TO WORSHIP

1. Organised Bible study taking place in small groups led by individual leaders or elders (examples in Liturgy Model One). As people walk into the church, they join any group or, if they wish, they may sit in a quiet place to meditate.

2. Singing of choruses led by an individual or a choir or a group of singers.

3. A time of reflection. This is where a leader/ elder leads those present to pray on specific topics or offers the opportunity for individuals to pray silently.

CALL TO WORSHIP

The minister or worship leader calls members to worship. One or two Scripture sentences may be used.

WELCOME

Once again it is my pleasure to welcome you all to God's house. We have gathered here as different people with one goal. We have come as individuals, but we are all one in the spirit of God. Feel at home with your God and fellow brothers and sisters in Christ as we worship Him in praise and in joy.

This kind of welcome or similar may be repeated during the time of notices. Extend greetings to all people but specially those who are attending for the first time. Request them to stand and let them introduce themselves. Also, enquire from the congregation if it is someone's birthday. Join together to sing "Happy birthday".

HYMN OR CHORUSES
(See list of choruses in appendix.)

OPENING PRAYER

Most gracious God, loving and caring Father, provider and sustainer of life, creator and maker of the universe; we have come before you in humility to ask you not to abandon us but to come and join us as we worship.

We thank you for yet another day.

We thank you for all the care and the blessings you have showered upon us all these years.

We thank you for the food we eat every day, the clothes you clothe us with every day, the air we breathe every day and the strength that helps us to recognise your presence with us every day.

We ask that you continue to fill us with your spirit as we engage with you throughout this sacred time of worship. In Jesus' name we pray. Amen.

(Followed by the Lord's Prayer)

HYMN

READING

A dramatised reading may be used.

(At the end of the reading)

This is the word of God

Thanks be to God

CHORUS

(See list of choruses in appendix.)

TESTIMONY

If you wish to introduce testimony time, announce this a week before to prepare those who wish to share their faith with others.

Invite individuals who want to thank God for what God has done for them. This could be a miraculous saving or deliverance or an answered prayer. Testimonies should encourage others and build up the faith of the whole church. They should be short and to the point.

PRAYER OF INTERCESSION

A mass vocal prayer. At this point the minister/worship leader offers members the opportunity to pray aloud. They are offered topics to pray about.

LET US PRAY

Let us join our hearts together and in our own time pray for others and ourselves. Let us ask God to continue to shower His love and blessings upon us and to protect us.

Feel free to pray in any language of your choice.

The minister or worship leader calls out the next topic when the praying ceases or becomes less vocal by saying the following.

1. *Let us pray for all churches in the world, but especially our own church and churches in this community.*

2. *Let us continue to pray for families: our own families who are facing trouble or divorce, those who are in danger, children and adults who suffer abuse at home, the sick and homeless people; those out of work and those looking for work.*

3. *Let us continue to pray for our countries, for our prime ministers, presidents, all leaders of nations, that they may strive to work for peace and justice.*

4. *Let us continue to pray for those who have died. Let us remember those families left behind, the widows and widowers, and especially the children left behind.*

5. (More topics could be added at this point if there is time to continue.)

The minister or worship leader may conclude the mass vocal prayer with the following, or words of his/her own.

Eternal God, we thank you for hearing our prayers. Continue to remain with us throughout our lives and especially the new week which we begin. Amen.

This kind of prayer needs to be timed to know when to bring in the next request.

CHORUS
(See list of choruses in appendix.)

READING
It is best to use a dramatised reading from the dramatised Bible.

(At the end of the reading)
This is the word of God
Thanks be to God

SERMON
Preaching the word.

OR

If the Bible study was used to start the service this may be used as a discussion point, using a flip-chart. Another approach is to refer to the Bible discussion/study (in model one), using a flip-chart to write down points during a brainstorm. The minister or worship leader concludes with a summary.

OR

A dramatised play by youths or a group of people.

PRAYER
End the section with a short prayer.

NOTICES

OFFERTORY

Members of the congregation may be invited to bring their offertory forward to a bowl placed in front of the altar. Lively music is played, or a chorus or hymn is sung while people dance to bring their offerings.

OFFERTORY PRAYER

HYMN

BENEDICTION

LITURGY MODEL FOUR

INTRODUCTION

This model is used when the majority of worshippers come from the same country.

The group is encouraged to prepare and lead worship as it is done in their country. The Women's Fellowship Group, Junior Church, Youth Groups or other groups in the church may be involved to lead worship. The group is guided by the minister when they are preparing the liturgy.

In this case the minister may preach the sermon or there may be a dramatised play by the group.

The teaching of new choruses from that country is also encouraged.

Groups may also be asked to lead special services as it is done in their country, e.g. harvest celebration, anniversary celebrations.

The model has a slot for a healing service. This kind of service is very important to most people in multicultural congregations. However, like all other services it must be planned very carefully.

HEALING SERVICE

SUGGESTIONS

This kind of worship should be occasional. It could be twice, thrice or four times a year.

The congregation need to be informed of this kind of worship in advance.

The healing service is a service that helps individuals to reconcile themselves with their past, heal past wounds, and forgive those who have hurt them (victims of rape, torture, divorce, abuse etc.). It is only God who can heal through others. Therefore the healing service is not necessarily to make the blind see or the lame walk. However, miracles could happen. This must be made clear to the congregation.

If one intends to have a healing service, it could either be in the morning with communion or in the evening.

LAYING ON OF HANDS

There should be a time during the service to invite individuals to come forward to be prayed for and hands laid on them. If the congregation is very big, the minister may ask some elders or leaders to join him or her.

ANOINTING WITH OIL

Scripture reminds us that we should use oil to anoint (*Psalms* 92:10) after laying on of hands. The minister uses oil to anoint the person by marking a cross on the forehead.

LITURGY FOR HEALING WORSHIP

If possible the setting of the room should be different on this occasion. Chairs may be re-arranged in a different form. Also encourage members to sit in different places if they have permanent sitting places. The most important thing is to encourage a sense of togetherness.

CHORUSES OR HYMNS OF PRAISE

WELCOME AND PURPOSE

We have gathered here this morning (or evening) *to be open with God to seek healing from him.*

We have come here to praise His wonderful name and first to put before him our shortcomings and to ask God for forgiveness. We will then put our request before Him. Our pain, our anger, our disappointments as Christians, our frustrations and all our burdens before God to seek healing. This may be physical or spiritual. In His own way God will show his powerful will to you. Therefore, relax and feel at home as we begin our service of healing.

SCRIPTURE READINGS

SILENT PRAYER WITH LEADING TOPICS

Let us remain silent and bring before God our shortcomings.

Give thanks to God for all his mercies and blessings.

Bring before God things you have done wrong.

Ask God to forgive you all the things you have done wrong and fill you with His Spirit.

(The Lord's Prayer)

CHORUSES OR HYMNS

TESTIMONIES

Invite individuals who wish to tell about God's abundant Grace and to thank God for what He has done for them through faith. This could be a miraculous saving or deliverance or an answered prayer. Testimonies should encourage others and build up the faith of the whole church. They should be short and to the point. This kind of testimony encourages others and ministers to them in many ways.

SCRIPTURE READINGS

PRAYER OF INTERCESSION

The Minister prepares the congregation for an open vocal prayer or, for those who wish it, to pray in silence.

Let us come together with one mind and one heart to pray for ourselves and others. You will be invited to pray aloud in any language or in silence during the prayers. Let's remain silent for a moment.

Silence is kept for a while. A hymn or a chorus is played by the organist.

The Minister reads out the topics to be prayed about.

Pray for the relief of pain for an individual that you know and for those you don't know.

Pray for children and parents who are suffering around the world, including your own country.

Pray for the homeless, the unemployed, victims of crime, victims of war.

Now pray for yourself and bring all your concerns before God.

Tell Him what you want and what you need.

Now let us pray together: Thank you Lord for hearing our prayers. We now with one heart and mind bring before you all children, men and women who are suffering in one way or other, who find it difficult to forgive those who have hurt them. Father God, help us as a community and also as individuals to show love and to realise that forgiveness brings healing. Let us accept any plea that comes from our neighbours when they realise their fault.

Receive our prayers through the Almighty power of the Holy Spirit, and unite us through your own son Jesus Christ our Lord. Amen.

Laying on of hands and anointing of oil.

At this moment, when the hymn or chorus is being played, invite those who need special prayers and laying on of hands and anointing to come forward. The minister and elders lay on hands and pray for them one after the other.

COMMUNION: THE TRADITIONAL WAY
This is optional.

The healing worship should end in silence if there is no communion. After the laying on of hands the minister leaves in silence. This is followed by the congregation in their own time.

DIFFERENT LITURGIES USED BY DIFFERENT ETHNIC GROUPS

The following are examples of liturgies used by the Kenyan, Ugandan, Tanzanian, Zambian, Zimbabwean, Mozambican, Botswanan, Mosotho, Swazi, Namibian, and South African communities. There are also examples from the Filipino community, Ghanaian community for Harvest celebrations, and a Junior Church celebration.

ORDER OF SERVICE

A liturgy to lead a multicultural worship was prepared by members from the above countries. Here is the structure. It may look traditional but the content is different:

1. Singing of choruses;

2. Call to worship, Psalm 1;

3. Music on tape, such as "Humble Yourself";

4. Opening prayer. A prayer said in any language to be followed by the Lord's Prayer in different languages;

5. Chorus: "Amazing Grace";

6. Prayer of Adoration (Chorus: Each member sings in own mother tongue – "Saviour Hear my Humble Cry");

7. Hymn: "When we walk with the Lord … Trust and Obey";

8. Prayer of Intercession. A hymn sung from Nyana Hymn book in Zulu/Bemba. Individuals pray in their own languages for

themselves, their families, their governments and heads of state, the sick and the their communities. This could be a silent prayer or a vocal prayer;

9. Brief history of the above countries to help others to know where their neighbours come from;

10. Hymn: "I need thee every hour";

11. Bible readings;

12. Reflections by minister;

13. Chorus: "Give me Joy in my heart";

14. Announcements and offertory. The offertory should be brought forward to be put in a bowl placed at the front of the church while lively music is played or a chorus is sung;

15. Closing hymn: "Guide me O thou Great Jehovah";

16. Benediction.

YOUTH AND JUNIOR CHURCH CELEBRATION/SERVICE

ORDER OF WORSHIP

1. Call to Worship: "Let the little children come to Me, and do not forbid them: for of such is the kingdom of heaven" (*Matthew* 19:14).

2. Songs of Fellowship or an appropriate song or chorus.

3. Prayers followed by the Lord's Prayer.

4. Prayer of Adoration: *Dear father of all creation, we adore and glorify your name. We magnify you and sing praises to you. You are our creator and provide us with all that we need. We have come together as your children to lift you higher above all generations. We have come because you called us, open up and hear what we bring to you and your people. Amen.*

5. Prayer of Thanksgiving: *Dear Father, we thank you for giving us this opportunity to bring your word to others in a different form. We thank you that we can share what we know*

with our friends, Mums and Dads. We thank you that the church has recognised us as part of the body of Christ. Shower upon us the gift of the Holy Spirit to inspire us to share Jesus Christ with others. Amen.

6. Prayer of Confession: *Most Gracious and loving God, you created us in your own image as children of today, to know you as we grow and to serve you. But our understanding of you is limited, our love for you is not perfect, we have disobeyed your instructions and gone astray. We have loved the world more than your word. Day by day we pay no heed to our mothers and fathers. But you never condemn us. We want to say we are sorry and never be angry with your children. Do not hold all the bad things we have done against us, but in your tender love receive us and forgive us in Jesus' name. Amen.*

7. The Lord's Prayer.

8. Introduction of theme of worship.

9. Songs of Fellowship or choruses from other countries in different languages.

10. First Bible reading.

11. Second Bible reading.

12. Sketch 1: Juniors. This could be a dramatised play from the Bible.

13. Reading a poem, or individuals are invited to sing in their own language.

14. Sketch 2: Seniors. This could be a dramatised play from the Bible.

15. Reading a poem, or a song by a group or individual in their own language.

16. Talk by one of the Youth based on the theme, or a message to fellow Youth or a story or a testimony.

17. Prayer of Intercession: *Dear God you care for all children, you know where each one lives, you protect us when we are in danger, you give us food, clothes, and all our needs. We have come to you today and ask you to hear our prayer. We pray for all children and young people of the world today, especially*

children and youth of this church. Guide us as we grow and let your Holy Spirit lead us wherever we go. We pray for children and the Youth whose lives have been ruined by drugs, alcohol and bad company. We pray for those who have been caught by the law and are imprisoned. Touch them and assure them of your presence wherever they are. We pray for our mums and dads and all those who bring up children, that you may give them patience and love in all that they do. We pray for the sick, both young and old, those who are suffering in many ways, that you may touch them with your healing powers to offer them relief. Father God, by the power of your Holy Spirit, we bring these requests before you, hoping you are here to hear them and act upon them in Jesus' name. Amen.

18. Reflection: Minister/Worship Leader

19. Notices.

20. Offertory: The congregation bring their offertory forward to be placed in a bowl, with lively music or chorus.

21. Hymn/Chorus.

22. Benediction: *Go out into the world with God's Blessing. Go out into the community in which you belong, your homes, your workplaces. And may the peace of our Lord Jesus Christ be and remain with you always. Go in peace and serve the Lord in Jesus' name. Amen.*

HARVEST SERVICE LED BY THE GHANAIAN COMMUNITY –
"KOFI AND AMMA" STYLE OF GIVING

This kind of worship is associated with harvest. Members are requested to give to God as much as they can offer to show their appreciation to God for all the blessings showered upon them. It is used as a fundraising worship. Normally envelopes will be printed and given out to members to put their donations in. Members are encouraged to take some envelopes to give to their families and friends and to invite them to their harvest celebrations.

After the envelopes have been collected, the "days of the week offering" is organised. This means that each and everyone should know the exact day they were born. This is known as "Kofi And Amma". It starts with Sunday-born to Saturday-born. The amount collected is counted and announced before the close of service.

The Ghanaian-style service follows a typical Reformed pattern of worship until the giving section in the service. This is styled as a "Kofi and Amma" service. The key feature of it is that members of the congregation come (dancing) forward to give in groups, according to the day of the week on which they were born ("Kofi" – boy born on Friday, "Amma" – girl born on Saturday). Each day's group gives separately. The Sunday-born come forward to give, and when they have finished, the Monday-born do so next, and so on. Non-Ghanaians need to be warned in advance that they will need to know the day on which they were born. After each day group has given, a rough count is made of the sum it has raised (it is helpful to get people to put their contributions in envelopes and write on the envelope how much is in it). The sums given by each day group are then announced. The chairman will then challenge each group to increase its total ("We've got £150 – can we make it £200?") and the whole church similarly ("Lets make it £1,000!"). There is a friendly rivalry between the day groups to see who can raise the most, but this is all done in fun. It is remarkable how much more money arrives if this period is allowed to continue.

In Ghana, some churches use "Kofi and Amma" giving at frequent intervals. It is typically done at harvest festival, where individuals will give to God to thank Him for all that He has done for them throughout the year.

In the following prayers etc., the congregation say the words in **bold** print.

Organ prelude and silent prayer. Entry of Bible (if it is the practice of the church) (all stand)

Call to worship (from Ps. 67)

> *Let the peoples praise you, O God:*
> **Let all the people praise you.**
> *The earth has yielded its harvest:*
> **God, our God, has blessed us.**
> *Let all the ends of the earth fear him.*
> **Amen.**

<u>HYMN or CHORUS</u>

<u>RESPONSIVE READING of PSALM 65:</u>
At the end, we say together:
> **Glory to the Father and to the son and to the Holy Spirit.**
> **As it was in the beginning, is now,**
> **And shall be for ever. AMEN.**

<u>TALK</u>
Children Address

CHORUSES

NOTICES – NORMAL OFFERTORY AND DEDICATION
Extend greetings to all people but especially those who are attending for the first time. Request them to stand up and let them introduce themselves. Are they visitors or have they just moved to the area? Offer them the opportunity after the service to meet an elder or a pastoral leader to take their details. Also, enquire from the congregation if it is someone's birthday. Join in to sing "Happy Birthday".

READINGS
- Old Testament
- New Testament

HYMN or CHORUS

SERMON or A DRAMATISED PLAY

CHORUS

INTRODUCTION TO "KOFI AND AMMA" SECTION
- Explaining what a "Kofi and Amma" service entails (as above);
- Explaining that in Ghana everyone has a name derived from the day on which they were born (men and women) and what the names are.

PRAISE

During this part of the service we praise and thank god using (some of) the following hymns/songs (which can be found in the appendix), not necessarily in the order below. During this period members of the congregation will be invited to come forward to give offerings according to their day of birth. Announce this:

Please put your gifts in the small envelopes provided, write on them how much is in the envelope, and (if you pay tax) complete the Gift Aid declaration.

- "Jesus put this song into our hearts"
- "Da n'ase (Thank the Lord for He is good)"
- "Yi n'aye (Worship Him, Worship Him)"
- "Halle-, halle-, halle-lujah"
- "Come on and celebrate"
- "We are marching in the light of God"

ANNOUNCEMENT OF SUMS RAISED

The sums raised by each day group are announced – opportunity for further giving, during which praise continues.

CLOSING PRAISE – RESPONSIVE READING OF PSALM 67

O God, be gracious to us and bless us:
Make your face shine upon us.
Let your ways be known on upon earth:
Your saving grace to every nation.
Let the peoples praise you O God:
Let all the peoples praise you.
Let the nations be glad:
And sing aloud for joy.
Because you judge the peoples justly:
And guide the nations of the earth.
Let the peoples praise you, O God:
Let all the peoples praise you.
Then the land will yield his harvest:
God, our God, will bless us.
God will bless us:
And the entire world will fear him.

HYMN or CHORUS

BENEDICTION

ADDITIONAL PRAYER

The following collective prayers may be used in addition to what has been written by the group leading the worship.

INVITE MEMBERS TO PRAY

We have come together in the sight of our redeeming God to bring to Him through the Holy Spirit ourselves and our worship, our praise and our thanksgiving; to confess our sins; and to ask our Saviour on behalf of all people our daily needs.

Let us pray.

OPENING PRAYER

Parent and everlasting God, the one who knows every movement of our lives, we adore and worship you. We ask that even though we cannot see you face to face, you grant us grace and mercy so that we may always cling to you with faith. Help us in our endeavour to know you better every day, and to love you more through our Lord Jesus Christ.

CONESSION OF SIN

Let us confess our sins to God.

O Holy and loving God, who knows the heart of every individual and tests our conscience, we humbly and genuinely admit our personal faults and failures:

Lord, pardon us.

For greed, envy, pride, and lust:

Lord, pardon us.

For many other sins which we have committed knowingly or unknowingly and where we have driven many into misery:

Lord, pardon us.

Let us now in repentance confess the sins of our previous leaders, sins of our age and our nations, admitting our share in them:

Lord, pardon us.

For racial hatred, prejudice, gender discrimination, jealousy, belittling one another and bitterness:

Lord, pardon us.

For broken marriages, child abuse, domestic violence, neglect of our duties as parents:

Lord, pardon us.

For immoral conduct, violence against weaker nations, inciting wars, industrial disputes which create unemployment that breeds hardship:

Lord, pardon us.

Parent and forgiving God, when you have pardoned our sins, and washed us with your clean Living Water, humble our hearts and make us holy and able to carry your cross to a better way of life in this world through your only begotten son Jesus Christ.

Parent God, protect us and set us free from the power of the evil one, and keep us under your umbrella. Continue to protect us from all principalities of this world and fill us with your Holy Spirit. Let your mighty hand and outstretched arm be our guard, in mercy and love through Jesus Christ our Saviour.

And let your word be light and instruction to our feet throughout the days and years to come.

Amen.

WE HAVE A DREAM

U.S.A. (ROBERT HENRY EARNSHAW)

We have a dream

1. We have a dream, we have a dream
This nation's folk both black and white
Will sit together at the feast
As sons and daughters in God's sight

2. We have a dream, we have a dream
That North and South, both rich and poor
Will hear the message of the Christ
That all must share God's harvest store

3. We have a dream, we have a dream
That from the mountain of despair
A stone of hope can still be hewn
To build a land that's just and fair

4. We have a dream, we have a dream
That love and justice have no bounds
Harmonious songs will soon transform
This nation's wild discordant sounds

5. For Christ has called us to be one
Let barriers now be broken down
Let freedom ring from every hill
In every village, every town.

ROUND TABLE CHURCH

U.K. (FRED KAAN. TUNE: HOLY LANE, PAMELA WARD)

The church is like a ta- ble, a ta- ble that is round. It
has no sides or cor- ners, no first or last, no ho- nours; here
peo- ple are in one- ness and love to- ge- ther bound.

1. The church is like a table,
   A table that is round.
   It has no sides or corners,
   No first or last, no honours;
   Here people are in one—ness
   And love together bound.

2. The church is like a table
   Set in an open house;
   No protocol for seating,
   A symbol of inviting,
   Of sharing, drinking, eating;
   An end to them and us.

3. The church is like a table,
   A table for a feast
   To celebrate the healing
   Of all excluded—feeling,
   (While Christ is serving, kneeling,
   A towel round his waist).

4. The church is like a table,
   Where every head is crowned.
   As guests of God created,
   All are to each related;
   The whole world is awaited
   To make the circle round.

MANY AND GREAT

U.S.A. (NATIVE TRADITIONAL)

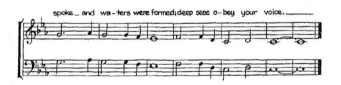

1. Many and great, O God, are your works,
   Maker of earth and sky;
   your hands have set the heavens with stars;
   your fingers spread the mountains and plains.
   You merely spoke and waters were formed;
   deep seas obey your voice.

2. Grant us communion with you, our God,
   though you transcend the stars.
   Come close to us and stay by our side:
   with you are found the true gifts that last.
   Bless us with life which never shall end,
   eternal life with you.

JESU TAWA PANO

ZIMBABWE.

Jesu tawa pano;
Jesu tawa pano;
Jesu tawa pano;
tawa pano mu zita renyu.

Jesus, we are here;
Jesus, we are here;
Jesus, we are here;
we are here for you.

MOMMA NO SO

GHANA. (HARMONY: P. BARKER)

Twi Momma no so IM

JESUS is king, give him all the glory;
Jesus is king, give him all the glory;
Jesus is king, spread abroad his story,
 He is Lord of all.
He's king of kings, and Lord of lords, so bow down now
And give him honour, thanks, and praise;
He's king of kings, and Lord of lords, so bow down now
And give him honour, thanks, and praise.

KYRIE ELEISON

U.S.S.R.

Kyrie eleison.

Lord, have mercy.

HE CAME DOWN

CAMEROON.

1. He came down that we may have love;
   he came down that we may have love;
   he came down that we may have love,
     hallelujah for evermore.
       (repeat verse)

2. He came down that we may have peace;
   he came down that we may have peace;
   he came down that we may have peace,
     hallelujah for evermore.
       (repeat verse)

3. He came down that we may have joy;
   he came down that we may have joy;
   he came down that we may have joy,
     hallelujah for evermore.
       (repeat verse)

HALLE, HALLE, HALLE

CARIBBEAN.

Halle, halle, halle — lujah!
Halle, halle, halle — lujah!
Halle, halle, halle — lujah!

YI N'AYE

GHANA. (HARMONY: S. G. BOATENG)

Twi   Yi n'ayɛ

WORSHIP him, worship him,
Worship the Lord;
Because he's good,
And his mercies never end.

translated from the Twi

SANTO

ARGENTINA.

quietly and steadily

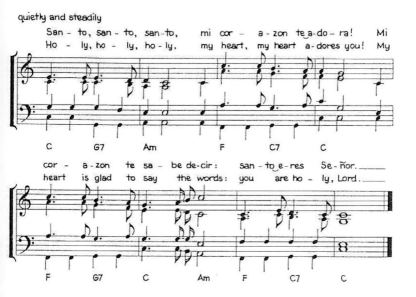

San - to, san - to, san - to, mi cor - a - zon te a-do - ra! Mi
Ho - ly, ho - ly, ho - ly, my heart, my heart a-dores you! My

C   G7   Am   F   C7   C

cor - a - zon te sa - be de-cir: san - to e-res Se - ñor.
heart is glad to say the words: you are ho - ly, Lord.

F   G7   C   Am   F   C7   C

Santo, santo, santo,
mi corazon te adora!
Mi corazon te sabe decir:
santo eres Senor.

Holy, holy, holy,
my heart, my heart adores you !
My heart is glad to say the words:
you are holy, Lord.

COME NOW, O PRINCE OF PEACE

KOREA. (GEONYONG LEE)

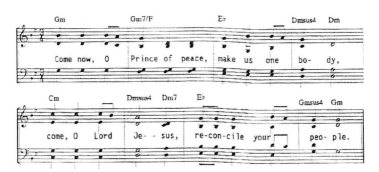

1. Come now, O Prince of peace,
   Make us one body,
   Come, O Lord Jesus,
   Reconcile your people.

2. Come now, O God of love,
   Make us one body,
   Come, O Lord Jesus,
   Reconcile your people.

3. Come now and set us free,
   O God, our Saviour,
   Come, O Lord Jesus,
   Reconcile all nations.

4. Come Hope of unity,
   Make us one body,
   Come, O Lord Jesus,
   Reconcile all nations.

1. O-so-so o-so-so,
   Pyong-hwa-ui-im-gum,
   U-ri-ga han-mom
   I-ru-ge ha-so-so.

2. O-so-so o-so-so,
   Sa-rang ui-im-gum,
   U-ri-ga han-mom
   I-ru-ge ha-so-so.

3. O-so-so o-so-so,
   Cha-yu ui-im-gum,
   U-ri-ga han-mom
   I-ru-ge ha-so-so.

4. O-so-so o-so-so,
   Tong-il ui-im-gum,
   U-ri-ga han-mom
   I-ru-ge ha-so-so.

WE ARE ONE BIG HAPPY FAMILY

KIRIBATI. (NGAIRA TEUANA: TRADITIONAL)

We are one big happy family,
God's family,
God's family.
We are one big happy family,
God's family are we.

She is my sister,
He is my brother,
Our Father in heaven,
He loves you and me.

Ngaira teuana te utu ae kakukurei,
Ana utu te Atua,
Ana utu te Atua.
Ngaira teuana te utu ae kakukurei,
Ana utu te Atua ngaira.

Neiei ai tariu,
Teuae ai maneu,
Ao tamara are i karawa,
E tangirai ma ngkoe.

This song was taught at the 1989 CWM Council Meeting in St Andrew's,
Scotland by the participants from the Pacific.

SARANAM, SARANAM (PSALM 61)

INDIA. (D. T. NILES: ARR. SHANTI RASANAYAGAM)

slowly, with dignity

Chorus
> Jesus, Saviour, Lord, Lo to Thee I fly;
> Saranam, Saranam, Saranam,
> Thou the Rock, my Refuge that's higher than I:
> Saranam, Saranam, Saranam,

1. In the midst of foes I cry to Thee,
   From the ends of earth wherever I may be,
   My strength in helplessness, O answer me:
   Saranam, Saranam, Saranam.

2. In Thy tent give me a dwelling place,
   And beneath Thy wings may I find sheltering grace
   O lift on me the sunshine of Thy face:
   Saranam, Saranam, Saranam.

3. O that I my vows to Thee may pay,
   And that by Thy faithfulness to me each day
   May live, and on Thy love my burdens lay:
   Saranam, Saranam, Saranam.

4. Yesterday, today, for e'er the same,
   Lo, the heritage of all who bear His name
   To ransom them from sin the Saviour came:
   Saranam, Saranam, Saranam.

O LET THE POWER FALL ON ME

CARRIBEAN. (BIRCHFIELD AYMER: TRADITIONAL
ARR: PATRICK PRESCOD)

1. O let the power fall on me, my Lord
   Let the power fall on me;
   O let the power from heaven fall on me,
   Let the power fall on me.

2. For we want power to live as one, yes Lord,
   We want power to live as one;
   So as we pray and intercede for some,
   May the Spirit make us one.

3. Send us the promised Comforter, O Christ,
   Send us the promised Comforter;
   And let our hearts be filled with love, O Christ,
   When the Spirit come like Dove.

4. Give us the power here and now, O Christ,
   Please for the power here and now;
   Send us the power of grace and peace and love,
   Send us the power of peace and love.

YEDA W'ASE

GHANA. (HARMONY: S. G. BOATENG)

Yeda w'ase, Nyame guammaa IM

LAMB of God, we praise your name;
u.never change, you're still the same.
u took away our sin and stain,
lamb of God, we praise your name.

translated from the Twi

YOU ARE THE TRUE KING

SAMOA. (ARR: K SARAGI)

1. We praise you O Christ Jesus,
   You are the only King.
   You rule your world in justice,
   Of Your great pow'r we sing.
   O come to us, Christ Jesus,
   The Prince of Peace you are,
   And hasten in your Kingdom
   For people near and far.

   Chorus
   Lord, bring in your reign,
   O yes Lord, bring in your reign,
   May your love and peace among us
   Now and evermore remain.

2. Make real your rule in Europe,
   America embrace.
   May north and south embody
   Your gift of love and grace.
   We pray, O Lord, for Asia,
   Its nations, one by one,
   Lead them into your fulness
   And may your kingdom come.

3. We pray that Madagascar
   And Africa's great lands
   Be drawn towards your presence
   And guided by your hand.
   New Zealand and Australia,
   Their peoples made by you,
   Their parliaments and leaders,
   In them your love imbue.

4. Lord, gather all the countries
   Spread out across the earth,
   The lands beyond the oceans,
   The world you've known from birth.
   Count China and Malaysia,
   New Guinea and Japan
   As members of your family.
   Bring in your loving plan.

5. Lord, bring in all the leaders,
   All governments and kings.
   May they bow down before you,
   To you their praises sing.
   In sacrifice and worship,
   In service to your name,
   We welcome in, Lord Jesus,
   Your everlasting reign.

GLORIA

PAPUA NEW GUINEA. (WOLFI SAUSI.

PARA: GWEN AND BERNIE COLLINS)

Guitar (Capo on 1st fret)

1. Ona long Papa na long Son na Holi Spirit
   God Triwan mipela sing long yu.
   Gut taim long ol man I laikim gutpela pasin
   God Triwan mipela ting long yu.

   Chorus
   Mipela i sing long yu,
   Presim yu na hamamas,
   God Triwan mipela sing long yu.

2. San mun na ol sta, klaut na blk solwara
   God Triwan ol i bilas b'long yu.
   Maunten na wara, flawa, animal na man
   God Triwan ol i adorim yu.

1. Honour the Father and the Son and Holy Spirit;
   Three in One, we sing our song to You.
   Peace to all people who rejoice in love and goodness.
   Three in One, our thoughts are full of You.

   Chorus
   We all sing our song to You,
   Praising You and sharing joy.
   Three in One, we sing our song to You.

2. In sun and moon and stars, in clouds and in the oceans,
   Three in One, we see Your beauty, Lord.
   Mountains and rivers, flowers, animals and people,
   Three in One, by these You are adored.

O HOLY SPIRIT

NIGERIA. (SAMUEL SOLANKE)

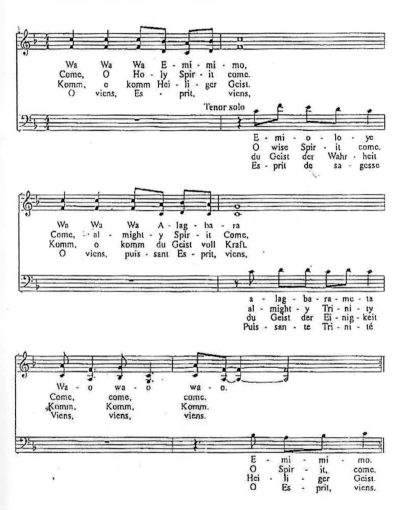

GOD WILL TAKE CARE OF YOU

SOLOMAN ISLANDS. (CIVILLA D. MARTIN,
W STILLMAN MARTIN)

1. Kalavarae koe Tamasa,
   Tataru nigo Sa.
   Korapa kopu nigo Sa
   Tataru nigo Sa!

   Chorus
   Tamasa kaqu koa,
   Ene kapae pa mua kinoa.
   Kaqu kopu nigo
   Doduru totoso.

2. Tutuvia goi talotana?
   Tataru nigo Sa.
   Tata mate, ke, nunala?
   Tataru nigo Sa!

3. Be noma mua tinavete,
   Tataru nigo Sa.
   Kaqu valeanigo Asa,
   Tafaru nigo Sa!

1. Be not dismayed whate'er betide,
   God will take care of you;
   Beneath His wings of love abide,
   God will take care of you.

   Chorus
   God will take care of you,
   Through every day,
   O'er all the way;
   He will take care of you,
   God will take care of you.

2. No matter what may be the test,
   God will take care of you;
   Lean, weary one, upon His breast,
   God will take care of you.

3. Through days of toil when heart doth fail,
   God will take care of you;
   When dangers fierce your path assail,
   God will take care of you.

ENTER INTO JERUSALEM

JAMAICA. (RICHARD HO LUNG. ARR: P. PRESCOD)

2. Enter into Jerusalem, mek we walk a–down there
With the young and the old, with the little and the large,
Mek we walk a–down there.
Enter into Jerusalem, mek we walk a–down there
Swaying to the breeze with the God who reigns in peace,
Mek we walk a–down there.

Chorus
We go celebrate, we go celebrate, we go celebrate, O Israel!
Praise the name of the Lord on high, praise His name in song.
Praise the Lord with a heav'nly song, with a heav'nly song,
With a heav'nly song praise the Lord.

3. Enter into Jerusalem, let us go to God's house
With your papa and your mama, with your uncle and your aunt,
Let us go to God's house.
Enter into Jerusalem, let us go to God's house.
Run and catch the breeze with the God who reigns in peace,
Let us go to God's house.

JESUS, WHERE CAN WE FIND YOU?

JAMAICA. (DOREEN POTTER)

1. Jesus, where can we find you,
   In our world today?
   Jesus, where can we find you,
   Incarnate Word today?

   Chorus
   Look at your brother beside you;
   Look at your sister beside you;
   Look! Listen! Care!

2. Jesus, in hand of the healer,
   Can we feel you there?
   Jesus, in word of the preacher,
   Can we hear you there?

3. Jesus, in mind of the leader,
   Can we know you there?
   Jesus, in aims of the planner,
   Can we find you there?

4. Jesus, in thought of the artist,
   Can we sense you there?
   Jesus, in work of the builder,
   Can we see you there?

5. Jesus, in face of the famished,
   Can we see you there?
   Jesus, in face of the prisoner,
   Can we see you there?

6. Jesus, in faces of children,
   Can we see you there?
   Jesus, in all of creation,
   Can we see you there?

RESOURCES

CWM, *Draw the Wonder*, CWM, 1995

David Peel, *Encountering Church*, URC 2006

Peter Ward, *Liquid Church*, Hendrickson, 2004

The CSI, *The Book of Common Worship*, 2nd Edition, Oxford University Press, 1962

The CSI, *The Book of Common Worship*, CSI, 2004

Vazhipaduvom, Dalit Resources Centre 2000

Many and Great, Songs of the World Church, Iona Community, 1990

Can I also draw your attention to the Council for World Mission songbook, *Drawn to the Wonder*, which has hymns from around the world, and the international song book from Iona called *Many and Great*. We have a number of songs from these books at the end of the book. There are, of course, plenty of others that could also be recommended.

John Danso is a member of the Urban Churches Support Group, which holds regular consultations concerned with "Rites of Passage". Not only do these consultations look at how different cultures respond to important moments in life, such as birth, marriage and death, the Urban Churches Support Group has also produced a collection of worship services and items drawn from different cultural traditions that have been tried and tested in the United Reformed Churches. Author's other book "The Ministry of Pastoral Care in Multicural Churches". These materials can be obtained from the United Reformed Book Shop.